WILD FLOWERS OF
THE CHANNEL ISLANDS

WILD FLOWERS OF
The Channel Islands

by

JOHN D. BICHARD
A.R.P.S.

and

DAVID McCLINTOCK

1975

CHATTO & WINDUS

LONDON

Published by
Chatto & Windus Ltd
42 William IV Street
London WC2N 4DF

*

Clarke, Irwin & Co Ltd
Toronto

47008416

ISBN 0 7011 2127 0

© John D. Bichard and
David McClintock, 1975

Printed in Great Britain by
Cox & Wyman Ltd
London, Fakenham and Reading

INTRODUCTION

For sheer rich variety of plants growing wild, the Channel Islands are without equal in England, Scotland, Ireland and Wales – which is one reason why visitors come from those, and other, parts. In all, about 1800 sorts have been recorded in the archipelago, an area of under 75 square miles. This is three or four times the average for Britain generally. The reasons for this richness of plant life are not difficult to find: the islands lie further south, with a warmer, milder climate, and have a good variety of habitats, where different sorts of plants tend to grow. They do not have every type of soil, for example pure chalk, but even so Jersey has some normally lime-loving plants in its northwest corner.

The dunes probably harbour more of the local specialities than any other area. Naturally the plants are mostly small, often very small, and it is a rewarding pastime to get down, carefully, and peer into the turf. There a remarkable variety of different plants will gradually be detected, including some rarities. In this sort of place will be found, for example (the numbers are those of the plants in this book) Atlantic Clover (22), Early Sand-grass (28), Bee Orchid (60), Hare's-tail Grass (63), Autumn Squill (71) and Autumn Lady's Tresses Orchid (93). In wetter turf are Sand Quillwort (23), Bog Pimpernel (74) and Slender Cicendia (75). More open, sandier ground and shingle may have Early Meadow-grass (12), Dwarf Spurrey (13), Mossy Stonecrop (14), Sea Radish (26), Variegated Catchfly (36), Grey Hair-grass (37), Sea Knotgrass (38), Yellow Horned Poppy (40), Great Sea Stock (41), Sea Kale (42), Jersey Thrift (44), Rosy Garlic (48), Sea Bindweed (61), Bermuda Grass (65), Deptford Pink (72), Vipers Bugloss (80), Fragrant Evening Primrose (82), Tree Lupin (83) and Rough Star-thistle (94). Cliff ledges will be a good place for Annual Rock-rose (33), Shaggy Mouse-ear Hawkweed (34), Greater Quaking-grass (39) and Lampranthus (69), and also on cliffs are Prostrate Broom (35) (often with Greater Broomrape (50)), Apothecaries Rose (55), Bell Heather (59), Golden Samphire (62) and Cape Cudweed (78). St Peter Port Daisy (27) is almost always on walls. On banks and in hedges grow Hedge Veronica (6), Large Lords and Ladies (8), ferns (9–11), Jersey Buttercup (17), Stars of Bethlehem (19, 20), Lesser Bird's-foot Trefoil (21), Bermuda

Buttercup (24), Balm-leaved Figwort (25), Greater Stonecrop (31), Ivy Broomrape (49), Wall Pennywort (52), Dew Plant (87), Wild Leek (92), Umbellate Hawkweed (95), Olearia (96) and Belladonna Lily (99). Look on wet ground for Marsh Dandelions (30), Loose-flowered Orchid (43), Giant Rhubarb (57), Dittander (58), Yellow Bartsia (84), Yellow Rattle (85), Galingale (90) and Green Cyperus (91). Waste ground and arable suit Field Marigold (32), Yarrow Broomrape (51), Salsify (54), Lesser Quaking-grass (64), Guernsey Canary-grass (66), Pimpernels (73) and Purple Vipers Bugloss (81). These lists include only plants in this book that are not otherwise mentioned in this introduction: and many of them will be found in other habitats than those given here: they have a good choice.

Changes in the use of land have also helped over 700 foreign plants to join the islands' flora, mostly during the past 100 years or so. They have their origins in many parts of the globe. A few examples from this book are Monterey Pine (5) from North America, Mexican Oxalis (88) from Central America, Cocks-eggs (56) from South America, Sea Fig (68) from Australia, Wire Plant (97) from New Zealand, Kaffir Fig (67) from South Africa, Gladiolus (53) from North Africa, Small-flowered Melilot (47) from India, Pencilled Crane's-bill (45) from the Near East, Winter Heliotrope (7) from Italy, Giant Echium (79) from the Canaries, Alsike (46) from Scandinavia, and others come from Madeira, the Caucasus, the Himalayas, China and Japan, and even the tropics.

These foreigners will have arrived in the course of trade and travel over the centuries. They will have come inadvertently on ships, vehicles and animals, with goods and packing materials, as well as adhering to clothing and even to travellers themselves. Many more will have come from gardens, their cast-out plants spreading from rubbish tips or by seed, or from deliberate planting. No-one can tell which plant they bring home will flourish and which will die. The fact that most of what most of us bring dies, is of small importance, for with just one successful, or over-successful, introduction, a species may well become part of the flora of the area. Such abundant, and beautiful, plants as the now execrated Stinking Onions (18) will have been originally in gardens, and still are, and welcome, in many further north. Agriculture and commercial horticulture are also responsible for many naturalised plants, above all the glories of the drifts and acres of most of the daffodils in the spring months (1–4).

The border line between what is and what is not a wild flower is nowhere harder to define than in these favoured islands, and is anyway ultimately a matter of opinion. In this book a wide view has been taken, recognising what people notice. Many would say that a Cabbage Palm (86) was not wild. This is very commonly and prominently planted. It flowers freely and bears fruits freely, and seedlings can and do come up in walls and other places and grow on on their own. The Guernsey Lily (100) is included largely for nostalgic reasons, for it is not now wild. Its intriguing story can best be read in a pamphlet called "The Guernsey Lily and how it came to Guernsey" written in 1970 by Miss R. de Sausmarez; and there is more on the subject in "The Wild Flowers of Guernsey" of 1975. Very briefly, this lovely South African species first flowered in the northern hemisphere in 1634, and in Paris; and yet 30 years later it was called in print the Garnzey Lily, as though that were its familiar name. In days gone by it was grown easily and in great quantity in the open there, and so it continued until some time in the last century. Then either the art of cultivating it was lost (as it was with Cape Heaths), or the stock deteriorated in some way. Nowadays it is to be seen only in greenhouses, and that rarely.

The native wild flowers of the islands are those which have, so far as we know (an essential caveat), been there ever since conditions allowed and have come in in natural ways. This by convention means unaided by Man – mammals, birds and the like are considered legitimate vehicles of introduction: anything coming with or by Man is not. But for sure many plants apparently native will in fact have arrived with undetected human aid. Were it not for historical knowledge, none would guess that some plants are in fact thus alien; and there may well be several in this book which few realised had come from far away and in quite recent times. What matters is that they are now part of the vegetation of the islands, fitting in with the other plants there and indeed adding richness and variety to the scene.

Connections with the flora of neighbouring areas are one indication of native plants, and the presumed natives of the Channel Islands have their nearest connections, hardly surprisingly, in north-west France. Consequently they have some plants, some in plenty, which do not, or hardly, grow in the rest of the British Isles. That the Channel Islands are politically British and not French is just one of those accidents of history. It can be argued that Britain belongs to them, rather than the other way round, for William, Duke of Normandy, owned them before he conquered England in 1066; and they are all that remain in English hands of his Dukedom.

The islands' plant specialities vary from the undoubtedly beautiful to what some refer to as the greens-and-dulls. The sand Crocus (15) is a plentiful example of the first – and it is invidious singling even this one out. Even more widespread, but not much to attract except under a lens, is what has lately been dubbed Guernsey Chickweed (29) by a witty visitor. Both are claimed as natives. All the plants mentioned in this book are natives, unless there is comment that they come from somewhere outside the British Isles. The existence, plentiful or otherwise, of so many special plants has brought hundreds, thousands, of visitors to these islands, many returning more than once. And so long as these flowers are allowed the chance, that is, they and their habitat are left in peace, so long will their beauty and interest continue for all to see and enjoy, and so long will these visitors go on coming.

That its habitat should stay right is the essential need for every plant to survive: no marshes, no marsh plants; no dunes, no dune plants and so on. Plants have become adapted over vast ages to certain surroundings and to be able to compete, or fit in, with other plants; and away from these conditions their life may be at best precarious. This is why all conservation must be based on maintaining suitable natural habitats. For where the right plants flourish, there will also be the right animals, mammals, birds, insects and other wild life. Plants are at the base of every food chain: no plants, no animals, no life. All this means conserving habitats not only by having nature reserves and the like, but much more by taking the greatest care, all of us, not to upset conditions. We should see that marshes and dunes do not get trampled – dune turf is particularly fragile and hard to repair. Where we have the control, we should cut or mow hedges or grass at the most beneficial time, and avoid draining naturally wet land – indeed by retaining or fostering the conditions the plants must have.

Inevitably, pressures and changes, which are all the greater in small areas, have caused the loss of certain plants. Some with a slender hold would probably have gone from natural competition in the normal development of the vegetation, but others have succumbed to human activities. Until the beginning of the last century Guernsey was divided into two by an arm of the sea westwards from St Sampson's called the Braye du Valle, which cut off most of the Vale parish in the north. When this was drained, to the great benefit of the island militarily and agriculturally, many of its salt marsh plants went too, for the island has few and small other areas where these can grow. In Jersey the drainage of St Peter's marsh, also in the last century, lost some marsh plants to the archipelago. These islands were two of the three places in the British Isles where the Summer Lady's Tresses Orchid could be seen; and seen it was by a long succession of plant collectors. It is now lost from all its known localities; and the Channel Islands have lost seven other Orchids in this century. In all there must be 50 or so flowering plants which are on record from the islands, which have not been seen for a long time. Some may reappear, some of them have. but most are gone for ever.

In sheer numbers however, the gains outweigh the losses. In the last hundred years or so there have been something like 700 new species recorded, mostly the introductions of all sorts mentioned earlier. Some of these are casuals, which crop up only occasionally, but many, most, are now part of the established flora. Some seem to have arrived, or been recognised, only very recently – Guernsey Fleabane (89) is one – and have already made their mark; and some are doubtless establishing themselves at this very moment: the process is endless. The astonishing Onion-grass (16) (which is neither an Onion nor a Grass, but a member of the Iris family) must have been where it is for many a long year before it was recognised, and it is otherwise unknown in the northern hemisphere. And the more closely people examine plants, the more new species and hybrids are they liable to detect – there are sure to be more of these to be added to the flora of the islands. So the grand total is always growing, from wider knowledge of native plants as well as from foreign ones newly established. It is particularly fascinating when a foreign plant manages to find a congenial niche in ground where the natives have been for so long entrenched.

There are apparent vagaries of distribution (that they seem vagaries to us merely reflects our ignorance of the causes) in the way many generally common plants (and animals) are to be found in one island and not another, or are plentiful in one and scarce in another. Some are not to be seen in the Channel Islands at all, plants such as Harebell or unplanted Marsh Marigolds. Jersey alone has, among others, Wood Anemone, Dog's Mercury, Greater Stitchwort, Bilberry and Golden Rod; Guernsey, Marsh Cinquefoil, wild Bugle, two Sedges and the only Wintergreen in the islands, now extinct; Alderney, Goatsbeard and Tor-grass; Sark is practically the only island in which to see Yellow Pimpernel (70); Herm has Heath Speedwell in plenty, which is at best rare elsewhere, and other plants in some quantity which are very rare in Guernsey close by. Hard Rush is on Jersey, Alderney and Herm, but not on Guernsey or Sark. Cow Parsley is in one small area on Alderney (perhaps planted), rare in Jersey, plentiful on the remote Ecrehos Rocks and nowhere else. Many other examples could have been given.

That remarkable woman, the Dame of Sark, who died in 1974 aged a lively 90, was ever helpful with her island's history, natural and otherwise. She wrote of it that "the wooded valleys in the spring are so thick with Primroses and Wild Hyacinths that the ground is flooded with a pale golden light or is as blue as the sky above. On every peak and headland great patches of gorse blaze brilliant yellow." So it is in the other islands, although few of us would have put it so well. In most parts of Britain the first flush of flowers is the supreme glory. But in the Channel Islands the climate allows also late flowers to flow on through the winter and early ones to break precociously; and not only in winter: Bell Heather for example is usually showing a red bell by May. And at the time when so many of the plants the Islands share with the Mediterranean are part of parched, shrivelled vegetation, most of the cover of the Islands will still be green, thus sharing the advantages of both the moist British and the sunny southern climates.

The choice of which flowers to include in this book was difficult. The first preference was for those with some special connection with the islands, either historically or by their distribution or in abundance. Some of these have very small or insignificant flowers, which attract chiefly the cognoscenti, and seemed therefore best left out; but some are in. Several of the special plants are grasses. Grasses do have charm, but are ignored by most people, so many otherwise suitable ones were passed over. After all, there was room for only 100. For these and other reasons the selection here is not just the chief specialities of the Channel Islands. But it is largely that, and ordinary British plants, however decorative, have been omitted. Those that are in, therefore, should help visitors to recognise many of the plants they will not be able to meet, or meet so easily, elsewhere in the British Isles.

The sequence of their arrangement is roughly seasonal. This means that in general those to be seen early in the year are in the early part of the book, and those flowering towards the end are at the end. But many of them show flowers for several months.

It should be said that the expression Britain is used to cover England, Scotland, Wales and northern Ireland. Ireland means all Ireland, British Isles all these plus the Channel Islands, which may be referred to as the Islands or the archipelago, for pardonable variation.

Those who wish to find out more about the plants of these islands should consult "The Wild Flowers of Guernsey, with notes of the frequencies of all species recorded for the Channel Islands" by David McClintock, Collins, 1975. A Flora of Jersey should soon follow, written by Mrs Frances le Sueur. Check Lists of the other main island groups have been published in the Transactions of La Société

Guernesiaise. That of Alderney was revised in 1974 and is obtainable from the Museum there. That of Sark appeared in 1963; that of Herm in 1961 and is still obtainable from the Guernsey Press. "Guernsey's Natural History" by N. Jee is an excellent account with more on the flowers. It is on sale at bookshops and bookstalls.

It remains only to thank two particular helpers. Mrs Patience Ryan, the Secretary of the Botanical Section of La Société Guernesiaise, gave much assistance in locating suitable plants for photographing and otherwise. Mrs Margaret Long, of the Botanical Section of La Société Jersiaise, sent photographs of four of Jersey's special plants (17, 33, 44, 81) and so saved journeys to that island, and helped with advice too. All the other photographs are by John D. Bichard, A.R.P.S.

November 1974   DAVID MCCLINTOCK

1. Guernsey Elm *Ulmus minor* 'Guernsey' and Daffodils *Narcissus* spp

Jersey and Guernsey Elms are very similar. Both have small leaves and stiffly erect trunks with branches rising steeply. This pattern shows best when the leaves have fallen. In this picture the tree is actually in flower – the flowers show as tufts of mauvish stamens on the twigs. The other Elm common in the islands, *U × hollandica*, has its trunk never erect, floppy branches and larger leaves. The two used to be known as the Male and Female Elms, although this implied no sex difference, and both have stamens as well as what develops into the green disc-like fruits. But neither sets fertile seed. They were brought from the Continent some hundreds of years ago and have been planted widely in hedges, where they may spread by suckers. They are an important part of the local scene and will remain so, subject to the effects of Dutch Elm disease. This photograph was taken in the Câtel in Guernsey at the dairy farm of Mr Nigel Jee, who first set out the characteristics of these two prominent trees.

Nor are daffodils native to the islands, except for the delightful Lent Lily, *Narcissus Pseudo-narcissus*, in Jersey, which makes open carpets, spreading by seed. All the others have been brought in for gardens or, in great quantity, for commercial horticulture. Those which were once grown, but were later rejected or superseded, now thrive on their own in fields and hedges, on cliffs and waste ground. The cut flower trade originated in 1864 when a consignment was sent to London by Mr C. Smith, who founded the Caledonia Nursery, which stocked the gardens of the islands for many decades. His enterprise inspired Mr Augustus Smith to start the trade in the Isles of Scilly. These horticultural varieties perfect very little seed, and very little, if any, of that germinates and develops into new plants in the wild. As a result, they spread solely by off-set bulbs, their clumps getting ever fatter and sooner or later breaking up; and all these daughter bulbs reproduce the original identically. Thus most of the millions of daffodils decking the ground are the spit image of those cultivated by past generations, a living museum of many dozens of varieties – well over 50 have now been named. Those in this photograph are 'Golden Spur', which is common.

I

2. Small-cupped Narcissi *Narcissus × Barrii*

These are the results of crosses first made nearly a hundred years ago. The parents were Large-cupped *N × incomparabilis* and Pheasant's Eyes, *N majalis*. The original forms had narrow "petals", that is, the outer parts of the flowers, whereas the prize-winners today have them broad and often overlapping. This one is 'Barri Conspicuus', which received an Award of Merit from the Royal Horticultural Society in 1886; and still cheers us as it cheered our forebears. Double-flowered varieties are about too. Their name comes from a great daffodil breeder, Peter Barr (1826–1909).

There are also plenty of Large-cupped Narcissi to be seen, single and double, hybrids between Trumpet Daffodils and Pheasant's Eyes, notably 'Carlton', 'Fortune' and 'Sir Watkin'.

3. Trumpet Daffodils *Narcissus § Pseudonarcissus*

These are what most people think of when they talk of Daffodils as opposed to Narcissi. Lent Lilies are the best known sort and wild in Jersey. 'Princeps', the one in this photograph, is often mistaken for it, but is larger and has the trumpet relatively shorter. It is an old variety, known at least by the 1830's and perhaps the commonest in the islands. It was grown for market, but has been long left to its own devices. Most of the other varieties in this section are not "bicolors", but have the trumpet and the "petals" of the same deep yellow – perhaps 'King Alfred' is the best known. The Tenby Daffodil, *N obvallaris*, also occurs, a plant connected with that town since at least 1825, but of uncertain origin. The early 17th century double 'Van Sion', the Cabbage Daffodil, was in the original hamper sent to Covent Garden in 1864 from Guernsey.

4. Tazetta Narcissi *Narcissus Tazetta*

Such varieties as 'Scilly White' and 'Soleil d'Or' are still much grown for Christmas in Britain, welcome not only for their early flowers, but for their strong fragrance. Tazettas will not do out of doors in most of the British Isles. In the islands however they find conditions to their liking and some, notably 'Grand Monarque' and the one in the picture, 'Grand Primo', are common in many places, perhaps best, like most of these daffs, in Guernsey. 'Primo', as it is usually called, is sterile, but nevertheless prospers vegetatively. It was known in the 18th century. 'Primrose Peerless', *N × medioluteus*, is at least 200 years older still, a cross between Poets, or Pheasant's Eye (the latter a much later name) and Tazettas, hence Poetaz. Pheasant's Eyes are also to be seen naturalised.

4

5. Monterey Pine *Pinus radiata*

This is native only in very restricted parts of the coast between San Francisco and Los Angeles, and is now far more abundant elsewhere in the world. It reached Britain in 1833 and is planted by the million in comparable climes. In the south-west of the British Isles it withstands winds magnificently and is a fine feature of the scenery – it forms the upper part of the Pine Forest in Guernsey. It has needles in bunches of three, grass-green when fresh. Its cones remain unopened for many years and can be seen stuck close to old branches and trunks even. Forest fires open them; so will less heat.

6. Hedge Veronica *Hebe × franciscana*

A wonderful plant for seaside hedging in climates such as that of the Channel Islands, which roots readily from cuttings and shows flower at most times of the year. It is a hybrid between two New Zealand species, which sets seed freely. The original seedling, 'Blue Gem', was raised in England in 1868, but was named scientifically only in 1943 at San Francisco – hence *franciscana*, the adjective for St Francis and for his city.

7. Winter Heliotrope *Petasites fragrans*

In the Channel Islands everyone calls this Coltsfoot, where surprisingly the yellow-flowered early spring plant known in most of the rest of the British Isles as Coltsfoot, *Tussilago Farfara*, is rare. This species is native in Italy and was not introduced until the beginning of the last century. The islands were some of the first places where it was reported wild, in the 1830's.

8. Large Lords and Ladies *Arum italicum*

The common Lords and Ladies, *A maculatum*, is not usually the common species in the islands. It is unknown in Alderney and Herm, where all the plants are of this larger species, rare in Britain, and the less common of the two in Jersey. This large species can be told for sure in the last three months of the year, when alone it will have its leaves, which sometimes have attractive yellowish veins, above the ground. It is also somewhat larger and flowers rather later with a usually yellow spadix, that is the curious central organ enfolded by the green sheath, which bears at its base the minute flowers. The tip is warm to the touch when it opens, much warmer than the surrounding air.

7

6

8

9. Lanceolate Spleenwort   *Asplenium Billotii*

A tufted fern of shady hedgebanks hardly to be seen in most of the rest of the British Isles, and not common even in the extreme south-west. Its fronds are usually about 6″ long, but some lush plants have them a foot or more. It is often overlooked for the also plentiful Black Spleenwort, *A Adiantum-nigrum*, but that has triangular, usually thicker, fronds on longer stalks. This one has also the habit of curving its fronds downwards at the tip and sides, especially when they are young. They mature later and are more wintergreen and so in better condition early in the year. It is quite frequent in the two larger islands, scarce in the others.

10. Guernsey Spleenwort   *Asplenium × sarniense*

Nowhere in the world has this hybrid fern been seen except in Guernsey, where it was found, new to science, only in 1971. It is a worthy quarry in the other islands, although they have fewer of the shady ivy-clad banks that it seems to like best, with its parents close by, often intermingled. These parents are the two species mentioned in the last account. It usually looks more like Black Spleenwort, but some forms are more obviously intermediate. Expertise is required to be sure of it, the final test needing a microscope to see if the spores are sterile.

11. The Guernsey Fern   *× Asplenophyllitis microdon*

Another great speciality, another, hybrid, sterile, fern of which only one example has ever been reported outside Guernsey, and that was 120 years ago, in the year after the first was seen in Guernsey. Again no-one has got it in the other islands, whereas over 20 tufts are known in Guernsey at present, about as many as of the last species, and no doubt others await discovery on some barish shady lane banks. Both this and the last plant should be photographed only and local botanists told about them, so that they may ensure their safety from inadvertent roadside tidiers. The cumbersome scientific name denotes this plant as that unusual phenomenon, a hybrid between species usually put into different genera, in this instance Lanceolate Spleenwort again and Hart's-tongue *Phylittis Scolopendrium*.

II

12. Early Meadow-grass   *Poa infirma*

Why this should be called infirm is a puzzle, for it can grow into thick tufts in good soil, although naturally it is smaller in dry places. Indeed it is just the same size as that of the ubiquitous weed, Annual Meadow-grass, *P annua*, from which it was clearly distinguished as a British plant only in 1914. Yet it is plentiful in many places of all sorts, roadsides, turf and so on. Usually it gives itself away by its pale yellow-green (infirm?) colour, but the common Annual can be similar. So then one has to look for the erect branches to its flower spikes and, for the really expert, its tiny anthers. Outside the Channel Islands it is known only in our extreme South-west.

13. Dwarf Spurrey   *Spergula arvensis* var *nana*

A variety, perhaps the ancestral form, of the weed of arable, common especially on sandy soils; and yet it was once used for fattening live stock and even humans – it was one of many such "weeds" eaten by Tollund Man shortly before his ritual death. This variety however is no weed of culture, but surely an ancient native of dune turf and cliff tops. It flowers before the weed starts and can whiten the ground with the stars on its short prostrate stems. Intermediates occur to the tall weed, but in its typical dwarf form it is a particular, and fragrant, early delight.

14. Mossy Stonecrop   *Crassula Tillaea*

Bare ground, usually sandy, is the place to see this brilliant beauty, not that it is always the colour in the photograph, or always in such fine patches. It starts life green, and it is only as it is ripening its seeds in the autumn of its life, in May, that it takes on this fiery tint. Often there is only a single stem, like a thread of red cotton an inch or two long on the ground. A week or two later all will have shrivelled for the year, leaving only seeds in the soil to repeat the brightness all over again.

15. Sand Crocus *Romulea Columnae*

A warm sunny day in April or May will reveal how plentiful this wholly delightful bulbous plant is on the cliff tops and dunes of the Channel Islands: closed flowers are inconspicuous because of the almost camouflage colours of the outer side of their petals. And yet, abundant though they are in parts of the islands, they are unknown in the rest of the British Isles, except on Dawlish Warren in Devon, where they were first noted early in the last century. The first mention of them in the Channel Islands is as long ago as 1726, but they must have been bespangling the ground for many centuries before that. They are no good at all in normal English gardens.

16. Onion-grass *Romulea rosea*

This a South African, common enough there, its corms eaten there as were those of the Sand Crocus in Guernsey. It is naturalised in Australia and as far north as St Helena. And then in 1969 it was found at Cobo in Guernsey – not just a few plants, but a thick stand of them 100 yards long with more near by, and all albinos. It is practically unknown in gardens and it is anybody's guess how it got there. But clearly it has made itself at home and is there for keeps, its only known occurrence in the northern hemisphere. It too flowers in April and May.

17. Jersey Buttercup *Ranunculus paludosus*

Paludosus means marshy, and yet this plant will be in flower on an apparently dry bank. The explanation is that this same bank or slope will probably have been very wet in winter, a fact realised, by Mrs le Sueur in Jersey, only recently. It was found in that island just over 100 years ago, and this is still the only place to see it, although it could be on other islands, overlooked partly because it is an early flowerer. It differs from Meadow Crowfoot by being shorter and unbranched, and underground it spreads by tubers on long string-like shoots. May is when it is out.

5

6

17

18. Stinking Onions   *Allium triquetrum*

What an offensive name for so delicately beautiful a flower – it is also called Wild Garlic, and even White Bluebells, but it is no Bluebell. The trouble is that most people become blinded to the beauty of abundant weeds; and this Mediterranean Onion is now ubiquitous in the islands: it started in Guernsey and was already abundant in 1847, source unknown, but doubtless a discerning plantsman unaware of how it would spread. People who come in July will see none of it, for soon after it has finished flowering it vanishes, leaving just its succulent bulbs in the hedgerows and roadsides. But earlier visitors should not fail to savour the chintzy charm of its waxen bells.

19. Star of Bethlehem   *Ornithogalum umbellatum*

A starry-flowered plant indeed, in full sun, which comes from further south and can spread in and from gardens in warm dry places, and can naturalise, for a while any way. Its flowers have pointed petals in a flattish umbel on a thick stalk, and its narrow leaves a prominent white stripe down the middle. The generic name means birds' milk in Greek and may refer to a similarity of the flowers to – bird droppings.

20. (Guernsey) Star of Bethlehem   *Allium neapolitanum*

The English name had to be set out thus, because this is the plant known in the Channel Islands as plain Star of Bethlehem. Starry it too is, like the last. But its flowers have rounded petals in globular heads on long thinner stems, and all green leaves. It was grown at one time for cut flowers; and what now decorates some hedgebanks are the naturalised descendants of these welcome Mediterranean, Neapolitan indeed, bulbs. Some detect they are sweet-scented too.

18

19

20

21. Lesser Bird's-foot Trefoil   *Lotus subbiflorus* (*hispidus*)

This annual is not rare in the islands, and yet it is always a pleasure to come across its orange flowers and shaggy foliage on some warm bank. It can grow to some size – it was measured at 2′ 6″ not long ago, but is usually under 6″. Also in the islands, but much rarer and more elusive, is the Least Bird's-foot Trefoil, *L angustissimus*, which differs most markedly in its pods, very long and thin for so small a plant, at least 1″. It is also less shaggy. The prominent fruit pods in this picture are those of Common Bird's-foot, *Ornithopus perpusillus*. The Orange-flowered Bird's-foot, *O pinnatus*, is a speciality of Guernsey, Alderney and Herm.

22. Atlantic Clover   *Trifolium occidentale*

White, Dutch, Clovers vary enormously. Some are lush and large, some small and wiry. But all seemed to be just varieties of *T repens* until 1961, when, after four years study the quite distinct species in this photograph was formally named. It is now known to grow, always close to the coast, from Cornwall to North Spain and Portugal. Nor is it rare in the islands. It is characterised by its small leaflets being always opaque when held up to the light and only extremely rarely with any markings. It is always prostrate, the stems often in rather typical curves. The time to be most sure of it is in early May, when it alone is in flower, three weeks before the common White Clover starts. Later both are out together.

23. Sand Quillwort   *Isoetes histrix*

A curiosity, a fern of sorts most of whose nearest relations grow in water. Admittedly this one needs turf which may be flooded in winter and which will even in summer have water not far below the surface, but its shiny curly overground "leaves" may be resting on quite dry soil. It is known in several places in Guernsey and a few in Alderney, but even more than the last, it is a plant one needs to get one's eye in for, and is likely to be undetected elsewhere including the other islands. The way to be sure of it is to lever it up carefully and see if there is a close sheaf of white leaf bases below ground, and then to push it back again.

24. Bermuda Buttercup *Oxalis pes-caprae*

In the Channel Islands this is a demure well-behaved beauty – but not yet noticed in Sark. In other areas, such as the Isles of Scilly, the Mediterranean, or Bermuda, it is a rampageous weed, spreading by the small bulbils it produces plentifully underground. The plant came originally from none of these places but, like most of its genus, South Africa. In few parts of the British Isles is the climate clement enough for it to survive out of doors. It is happiest on warm well-drained banks.

25. Balm-leaved Figwort *Scrophularia Scorodonia*

The photograph shows just the upper part of the inflorescence of this quite bushy plant, which may be 4′ or more high. Its first British record was from Jersey and it is the common Figwort of the hedges and bushy places in most of the islands. But it is not all that different from the two species common in Britain (but not so common, or even rare, in the islands) and consequently has been overlooked. It differs most obviously by having hairs all over the stems and leaves, which catch the dust, and in addition it has an untidier habit of growth. In Britain it can be seen as a native only in Devon and Cornwall. But what has prevented it reaching Alderney and Sark?

26. Sea Radish *Raphanus maritimus*

Here too only the top of the inflorescence is shown, but shows well the distinctive fruits, fat, 1–3-seeded, with a long point, which can float for several days in sea water. Otherwise it is very like a large, 2′–3′, longer-lived version of the annual weed *R Raphanistrum*, or indeed of our garden Radish, *R sativus*, both of which also occur in the islands. It is generally plentiful near the coast but has not yet been proved to grow on Sark. It is quite often heavily encrusted with snails.

24

25

26

27. St Peter Port Daisy *Erigeron mucronatus*

In St Peter Port it was that this delightful plant was first recorded wild, about the middle of the last century. No doubt it was originally brought from its native Mexico for gardens, where it still can be most welcome. It is at its most attractive on walls, where it quite often grows in profusion, and is only exceptionally to be seen elsewhere. It is at its best away from the sea and in the two main islands – it is not yet noted from Herm. Flowering goes on through much of the year, the flowers turning russet pink with age. It is now naturalised in several southerly parts of the British Isles.

28. Early Sand-grass *Mibora verna*

So charming is this small grass that it has been for many years in the catalogue of one of the leading British nurserymen. Its fresh green leaves come quite early and are good in any rockery, while the yellow stamens on its purplish inflorescences embellish it further. Thereafter it dries up and vanishes, like all good Mediterranean annuals. In the wild it can be quite plentiful, if not always immediately obvious, in dune turf and also on cliff tops, but seems not to be on Alderney or Sark – or have these islands not been properly searched early enough?

29. Guernsey Chickweed *Polycarpon tetraphyllum*

Here is a plant few would realise was special. But special it is, abundant in all the islands, very rare in England, abundant too in many sorts of places. As a weed of cultivation it can grow thick, well-branched and lush; on dry pathsides it will be small and thin. It is an annual, and really lacks a popular name, being a typical "weed"; but people come to the islands just to see such specialities. Most books call it, translating the Greek of the scientific name, Four-leaved All-seed, but the name above was recently produced and is much apter, except that perhaps Channel Islands Chickweed would be apter still. Ordinary Chickweed, *Stellaria media*, does occur too!

27

28

29

30. A Marsh Dandelion   *Taraxacum austrinum*

To most people Dandelions are just weeds to be got rid of. To a few they are flowers of rich beauty, which we would treasure if they were rare or difficult to grow. To fewer still they are an object of close study, for over 130 different species are known from the British Isles, 52 so far detected in the Channel Islands. Most perfect their seeds without cross-fertilisation. How to tell them apart calls for expertise, but the "Taraxacum Flora of the British Isles" of 1972 holds the key, and a fascinating study they can make – but are practically unnameable except in their main flowering season in spring and early summer. Only three species of the section called Marsh Dandelions are known in Britain, all scarce, but two of them grow in the Channel Islands. The one in the picture was taken at the Grande Mare in Guernsey and is also by St Ouen's Pond in Jersey.

31. Greater Stonecrop   *Sedum praealtum*

A large sprawling shrubby plant which can also grow into thick mounds 3′ high. It flourishes in gardens and portions root with no trouble at all. So it can be found managing outside them, in hedges and waste places: it has been known for half a century in Jersey. It is one of two similar species both of which come from Mexico, but are quite at home in the open in the climate of Jersey and Guernsey. It may also be seen, growing indoors, in Britain too.

32. Field Marigold   *Calendula arvensis*

This clear photograph should make it possible to tell this Marigold from the Pot one, *C officinalis*, so easily grown in gardens – for both may appear naturalised, the Pot one usually near garden rubbish heaps. Both are Mediterranean. This one is the larger plant, to 18″ or so high, with many more, smaller, flowerheads, always orange. It is now locally quite common in cultivated fields in parts of Guernsey, but has apparently not reached the other islands. Yet it is a persistent weed in one garden in Kent. Its remarkable fruits are like curly prickly small caterpillars.

33. Annual Rock-rose   *Tuberaria guttata*

Like other members of its family, this plant sheds its petals before the day is out, but next morning fresh flowers appear and, when the sun is out, open. This can make it an elusive quarry late in the day or in dull weather, for otherwise it is rather an ordinary looking annual. The best place to look for it is on the western slopes of Jersey. There is also a small colony on the south cliffs of Alderney, not at all easy to find. But it is still there, as it has been since it was first found, in 1838, and doubtless for long before then; its first British record was from Jersey in the 1680's.

34. Shaggy Mouse-ear Hawkweed   *Pilosella Peleterana*

Another "Dandelion", some may exclaim, who lump all such yellow composite flowers together. And this is also extremely attractive, but never a weed, and it lacks the milky juice of a Dandelion. It is most like the Common Mouse-ear Hawkweed, *P officinarum*, which is generally scarcer in the islands, but this one has much more character – long shag on the leaves and stems, short stubby runners and these sun-like flowers. It is at its best on sunny rock ledges, and only rarely to be seen in Britain.

35. Prostrate Broom   *Cytisus scoparius* ssp *maritimus*

A glory of the south-western cliffs of Jersey, Guernsey and Alderney. Brooms may be seen in other places growing flat to get out of the way of the wind, but give them shelter and they will grow upwards. But these Brooms have been flattened so long by the wind on the cliffs that they are now permanently made that way, and their seedlings too remain flat. This sub-species has the added attraction of silvery hairs on the young leaves, which set off the golden flowers to perfection. In Jersey and Alderney this has a special Broomrape (50) growing on it and never, in the islands, on ordinary Broom.

33

34

35

36. Variegated Catchfly   *Silene gallica* f *quinquevulnera*

Joshua Gosselin (1739–1813) was a remarkable Guernseyman, who among many other achievements laid the foundations of our knowledge of that island's plants. He it was who first mentioned this charmer, and who coined its name. Distinctive it is, but in fact it is no more than an unfailingly appealing colour form of the shabby arable weed, Small-flowered Catchfly. In this form however the flowers look like velvet cretonne, thanks to the deep crimson spots suffusing much of the white petals. Plentiful it is not, but even so it is surprising it is known only from the two largest islands.

37. Grey Hair-grass   *Corynephorus canescens*

Grasses look much alike to most people, all the greater pleasure therefore for those who begin to discover the manifold variety and beauties they exhibit; about 166 have been recorded from the islands, some very rare and special. This one has a strange distribution – plentiful on the Quennevais in Jersey, but nowhere else in the British Isles nearer than the East Anglian coasts, and always rare. Its tufts of leaves are of an attractive grey with often a good pink tinge to them. Its flowers, distinctive enough technically, hardly enhance it when they have gone over.

38. Sea Knotgrass   *Polygonum maritimum*

Herm is famous for its shells, mostly well ground down. Two plant rarities have been known there too. This is one and needs protection from heedless visitors. It is a stouter perennial version of the weedy Knotgrass, *P aviculare*, of waste and arable, with broad whitish stem sheaths and thick bluish-grey leaves inrolled at the sides. It starts flowering much earlier than most books say, and is best seen in May and June before the sand begins to look like a battlefield. In most years it is not seen in England or Ireland at all, but here it is quite reliable. But it is NOT for picking.

39. Greater Quaking-grass   *Briza maxima*

A grass of such attraction that it is in several commercial seed-lists. The appeal starts when the young flowers have their purple bases, and continues as these fade and the florets open and dangle. Picked then, they will dry intact for the winter. It comes easily from seed on dry warm soils. It is a moot point if it is native in the archipelago, but it is established in several spots in the two main islands.

36

37

38

39

40. Yellow Horned Poppy *Glaucium flavum*

Another plant with fugitive petals, like other Poppies, but this one has by far the longest pods of any plant in the British Isles – they can reach 1′, and twist and curve in most decorative fashion. It was at one time quite common on the sandy beaches and shingle it likes. But its attractiveness, its relative fragility and the disturbance visitors inevitably cause – quite apart from such difficulties as the wholesale removal of its shingle or burying it beneath rubbish – have made it nowadays scarce, least so in Alderney. In Sark there is no suitable ground for it.

41. Great Sea Stock *Matthiola sinuata*

This too is much diminished, and seriously. In Jersey it was once plentiful in some parts of St Ouen's Bay; nowadays it is rare. In Guernsey it could be seen on the dunes all down the west coast: now it hangs on by its eyelids in two tiny spots, a sad state for the Great Sea Stock. It has not been seen in the other islands. The Common Stock, *M incana*, now decks various cliffs and quarry sides in the three main islands, but these plants derive from cultivation, however bright and fragrant they may, welcomely, be. Garnsee Violets, as such Stocks were called in those days, were first mentioned in print in 1578.

42. Sea Kale *Crambe maritima*

In happy contrast to the last two plants, here is a coastal one that seems to have increased in recent years in Jersey and Guernsey, and there is as much as there ever was in Alderney. The fact is the more remarkable with the prominent nature of this perennial. In flower its 12″–18″ mounds of white flowers are most attractive and its thick blue-grey leaves must lure any flower-arranger. But, bless them, they seem to have resisted the lure. This plant is the origin of the vegetable so delicious when blanched. But do not try to eat wild ones: they are beyond any amount of boiling.

40

41

42

43. Loose-flowered Orchid *Orchis laxiflora*

This mouthful of an English name is a direct translation of the Latin one. There is a better one in the local patois, meaning Whitsuntide, which is when this glorious treasure of the islands is in flower. But even that is not nearly good enough for so fine a plant. The trouble is that it does not grow anywhere in the British Isles except in Jersey and Guernsey, so there has hardly been any call for a name in English – for the local versions of French or French itself were spoken until not very long ago. Although there have been inroads into the wet meadows it likes, happily it does still grow in colourful quantity in some of them, notably in the south-west of Guernsey. But it can be seen down much of the west coast there, and in St Ouen's Bay in Jersey – it has been called the Jersey Orchid, but there is much less of it there. It can be anything up to 3′ high and a bright sight with its flowers of a unique vinous purple, very rarely pure white.

44. Jersey Thrift *Armeria alliacea* (*plantaginea*)

Still a locally plentiful rarity in the area where alone it grows in all the British Isles, also St Ouen's Bay in Jersey. The Common Thrift, *A maritima*, grows there too, but is smaller with narrower greyer leaves and flowers earlier. The flowering times of the two hardly overlap, but do so sufficiently for hybrids occasionally to be formed. But it has not yet been seen in Jersey with white flowers, which occur from time to time on the common species.

45. Pencilled Crane's-bill *Geranium versicolor*

Another flower redolent of 18th century embroidery – another name for it is Queen Anne's Needlework, although it has been in our gardens since at least the early 17th century. It is local in Jersey and rare in Sark, but has been known in some ten places in Guernsey. Two easy ones to see it are by the formal gates at Sausmarez Manor, where it has been for a century, and near St Andrew's church. It was first recorded in Jersey over a century ago too. Yet another English name for it is Painted Lady.

43

44 45

46. Alsike *Trifolium hybridum*

This is a clover which has been sown for forage since the middle of the last century. Like other agricultural plants, it can be found quite often persisting on field edges and road-sides, but not for long. In Guernsey, however, it has settled down and may be seen growing quite thickly on some of the dunes of the north-west, which seems not to have happened in Britain. Nor is it rare in Jersey, where a "wilder" variety with almost solid stems, instead of hollow ones, has also been seen. Alsike is a village near Uppsala in Sweden, whence it was imported. Uppsala was the town where Linnaeus worked who gave it its Latin name. But by "*hybridum*" he meant only that it was intermediate in looks between Red and White Clovers, which it is.

47. Small-flowered Melilot *Melilotus indica*

Here is another plant which is to be seen elsewhere in the British Isles only as a casual hardly persisting, but which is now well entrenched in Jersey, Guernsey and Alderney. How it arrived and got going can only be guessed, for this is not grown agriculturally. In Jersey it was more or less naturalised by 1903, but the only record in Guernsey until 1928 was one plant in 1894, and by 1901 only two plants had ever been recorded on Alderney. No Melilots are likely to be native in our islands; and this one stems from India but is now to be seen all over the world.

48. Rosy Garlic *Allium roseum*

A flower of undeniable beauty which deserves to be seen much more in gardens. But that is no reason to dig it up outside them and not to go to a nurseryman. It has been known in Jersey for over half a century, but in Guernsey only since 1957. There however it has prospered and now decorates some dunes and waste places welcomely. It is yet another plant from the Mediterranean which finds sufficiently similar conditions in the Channel Islands. It was brought from further south to Britain over 200 years ago. Some forms have only flowers in the umbel without any of the darker bulbils.

46

47

48

49. Ivy Broomrape *Orobanche Hederae*

Broomrapes obtain all their nourishment from their hosts and are one of our few sorts of entirely parasitic plants. This one grows on practically nothing but Ivy, *Hedera* – but can appear some distance from where the Ivy obviously is, the explanation being that the Ivy's roots spread far and it is to the roots that these Broomrapes' suckers adhere. Ivy Broomrape is scarce in Britain, but in the Channel Islands it is plentiful in Guernsey and Sark, in both of which it is the commonest species. The first record for it anywhere in the British Isles was made in Guernsey at the Château des Marais, which even then, 250 years ago, was known as Ivy Castle from the masses of Ivy on its ruins.

50. Greater Broomrape *Orobanche Rapum-genistae*

This is our tallest and stoutest species of Broomrape. It grows plentifully on the south-west cliffs of Jersey and Alderney, where it parasitises the Prostrate Broom (35): it does not do this in Guernsey, nor does it grow on ordinary Broom there or in the other islands. It can be striking, often many stems together, on these cliffs, which at that time, May and June, are particularly floriferous. The generic name means a plant that strangles vetches (but any parasite that kills its host has bleak prospects), its specific epithet that it is a Turnip of Broom, the Turnip being the thickened base of its stem. Hence its English name too.

51. Yarrow Broomrape *Orobanche purpurea*

A rare species in Britain, but to be seen in Jersey, Guernsey and Alderney, where it is perhaps the most frequent species. It is usually purple, as the Latin name says, but the two colonies in Guernsey, where this photograph was taken, are of these unusual, distinctive and attractive colours. Yarrow, *Achillea Millefolium*, is the usual host.

52. Wall Pennywort *Umbilicus rupestris*

A fleshy plant which has been taken for a Broomrape, but is no parasite. It is generally common, often abundant, chiefly on banks and walls. On the former it has been measured 2′ 6″ high; on the latter it can flower at 2″. Its leaves can reach 4″ across, but are usually about 1″. Ferns vary similarly in size with habitat. The round dimpled leaves are the source of its generic and some English names, such as Venus' Navel or Navelwort.

49

51

50

52

53. Gladiolus *Gladiolus byzantinus*

In the 1700's this was known, and grown in the Channel Islands, as the Constantinople Corn-flag, hence the epithet the great gardener Philip Miller then gave it. Its bulbs had been brought in for our gardens at the beginning of the previous century, but not from anywhere near Constantinople (Byzantium; Istanbul nowadays): its nearest relatives are in North Africa. It was grown at one time for the cut-flower trade; and what decorates occasional fields and hedges are the descendants of these, colourfully surviving on their own. Nowadays it is rarely cultivated, its harsh ruby-red flowers being found less agreeable than those of modern hybrids of South African species.

54. Salsify *Tragopogon porrifolius*

"One plant in a potato field on the road from St Sampson's Bridge to Bordeaux" in Guernsey in 1900. Who would have guessed that this biennial would have been found at Bordeaux harbour ever since, and nowhere else on the island, except as a rare relic of its cultivation as the excellent vegetable that it is. It would be worth cultivating for its flowers too, if only they stayed open in dull weather. It has been similarly long naturalised in Jersey and was for some time in Alderney. It is a native of the Mediterranean.

55. Apothecaries Rose *Rosa gallica* 'Officinalis'

Few would believe so gorgeous a flower could be wild in the British Isles. But so it is, in Guernsey. In the 1920's this and some other Old Roses were planted on a headland on the west coast in full face of the salt gales; and there they still are, having not only flourished, but spread and competed with the brambles and other native vegetation. About ten garden Roses can be seen in that island similarly naturalised, and there are some in at least Jersey and Herm as well. This is one of the most ancient varieties, having been cultivated and famous at Provins 50 miles south-east of Paris since at least the early 1300's. It may have been brought there from Damascus by a Crusader.

3

4   55

56. Cocks-eggs *Salpichroa origanifolia*

A fast-growing perennial with somewhat woody branches, which spreads far and forms loosely knit mounds of vegetation. So far it has been seen in these islands only in Guernsey. It was first noted in 1946, but is now a prominent feature locally, the cause of many an enquiry about its name. Its two chief haunts are north of the Grandes Rocques hotel, and by Les Dicqs 1½ miles to the north east. But it is also in three or four other places where it is more kept in check. It comes from the Argentine and has been grown in gardens and greenhouses, people lured perhaps by another of its names, the Lily of the Valley Plant. The "Cocks Eggs" are the whitish fruits, said to be edible.

57. Giant Rhubarb *Gunnera tinctoria*

This is of course no Rhubarb (*Rheum* × *cultorum*), although in its native South America its prickly leaf stalks are also eaten, peeled. It is of the same family as the inconspicuous Water Milfoils, *Myriophyllum* spp, and most of its own genus are dwarf plants. But two are most imposing giants and both are to be seen. This however is the commoner one in the islands and sows itself in wet places, in Guernsey at any rate. It is also in Jersey, Sark and Herm. It had reached Guernsey by 1851, only two years after its first introduction to Europe, and soon was much cultivated there. Its descendants can be seen in at least nine places. The photograph shows mainly the remarkable and distinctive inflorescence, which can be obscured by the huge leaves, here seen young and unopened.

58. Dittander *Lepidium latifolium*

This is a native plant of seaside marshes. But it was also for long cultivated as a condiment for its acrid root and peppery leaves (hence the alternative name of Pepperwort). Horse Radish, *Armoracia*, then was introduced and took over, and later imported peppers. It has been known down the west coast of Guernsey for 200 years, but is at best planted in the other islands. Its flowers are very decorative atop their 5′ stems. Dittander derives from Dittany, *Dictamnus*, which it used to be called, muddling it with this quite different European species.

56

57   58

59. Bell Heather *Erica cinerea*

Bell Heather is plentiful over much of the British Isles. No other Heather has flowers of such a great variety of fine colours. The Channel Islands have their good ones too, indeed unusually few are poor at all. Four from its bailiwick on the market are Guernsey Pink, Plum Purple and Lime – the last has leaves of a unique lime-green colour and came from Brecqhou. White-flowered plants have been seen in all the main islands, two from Sark have been lately propagated – just from tiny $\frac{1}{2}''$–$1''$ side shoots. Ling, *Calluna vulgaris*, can be good too – curiously it is not in Herm, and at least one rich purple one is cultivated.

60. Bee Orchid *Ophrys apifera*

If only it were larger, this would surely be one of the most exotic British plants, and it is always one to treasure. It has not been reported from Jersey or Alderney since the 1940's. In Guernsey it was thought lost in the 1960's, until a local photographer was found to have taken its picture, unaware of what it was or how sought after it was. It has been known in several places in that island, but at present seems only to be appearing in one of them.

61. Sea Bindweed *Calystegia Soldanella*

This is not rare in England, but is becoming less frequent as the sandy coasts have to withstand ever more visitors. It is the same in the larger Channel Islands – Sark has no sandy coast. A special interest is that we know that it grew, in Guernsey at least, thousands of years ago. Its pollen has been detected in the peat there, miraculously surviving and retaining the unique sculpturing of its outer coat, visible with a microscope, an evocative link with the long past.

62. Golden Samphire *Inula crithmoides*

These "yellow Daisies" belong to a plant which is rarely to be seen in plenty in the British Isles, but which is in all the four largest of the Channel Islands. In Guernsey indeed it seems to be actually on the increase, being in perhaps a dozen places on the cliffs, distinct in its narrow fleshy leaves and stiff stems. Samphire is a name used for other seaside plants, including the totally different umbellifer *Crithmum*, from which nevertheless this gets its scientific name.

59

61 60

62

63. Hare's-tail Grass *Lagurus ovatus*

Who says grasses are dull? This poppet is to be seen in quantity over wide areas of the dunes of western Jersey and of northern and western Guernsey. In Guernsey it has been known in those parts since at least the 1780's, but in Jersey it was sown in the middle of the last century. It was sown too in its only English station. This, and the fact that it has hardly been known in France nearer than 300 miles further south until quite recently, and other considerations, suggest that it is no native even in Guernsey. But that it is vastly appealing, whether 1″ or 12″ high, there is no gainsaying. It dries well too, loveliest undyed.

64. Lesser Quaking-grass *Briza minor*

A grass just as attractive as its Greater brother (39) and at its best when that has broken up. It was first recorded from Jersey nearly 300 years ago, but is rare there now. It was collected in Guernsey in 1774 – the specimen is at Kew, the earliest of any wild Channel Island plant. So this is at least of long standing in the islands. It is a, pretty, weed of cultivation and waste ground, and delightful in gardens. The perennial Quaking or Totter-grass, *B media*, is a rarity in the islands.

65. Bermuda Grass *Cynodon Dactylon*

It is uncertain just how long this grass too has been in our islands – it is widespread in warm countries the world over, often in lawns. In some it has taken over the name of Couch. In India it is Doob-grass. It has been in the Channel Islands since at least the 1830's, but was spotted in Alderney only in 1956. Grasses with such fingered (hence *Dactylon*) inflorescences have a peculiar fascination. This one is a mat-forming perennial reaching about 6″ high. Locally commoner is Crab-grass, *Digitaria sanguinalis*, a taller annual of open ground and path sides, native further south.

66. Guernsey Canary-grass *Phalaris minor*

Ordinary Canary-grass, *P canariensis*, appears wherever birds have been fed or their debris taken, for its seeds are perhaps the commonest food for small birds. It has its flowers in egg-shaped heads. This species, a weed of arable most frequent in Guernsey and Alderney and casual in Jersey, has been known in Guernsey since the 18th century, but is hardly ever seen in Britain.

63

64

65

66

67. Kaffir Fig *Carpobrotus edulis*

"Mesembryanthemums" were all put into one vast genus until the early years of this century, when they were split into 100 or so genera – and the total number of species, of very varying appearance, runs well into four figures. Most come from South Africa, hence the English name of this one: Hottentot Fig is another. The fruits, not often perfected in our climates, can be eaten. But vegetatively some species do well, rooting rapidly from cuttings and flowering profusely. This one can form thick heavy carpets draping the ground or hanging from the cliffs, wherever it has been planted or birds have taken viable portions. Its flowers are just as often pale yellow as pink.

68. Sea Fig *Carpobrotus glaucescens*

This much resembles the last, but has smaller always pink flowers, which are white at the base, and smaller leaves. It is the only species on Herm and frequent on Alderney. Neither this nor the last have yet reached Sark. It comes from Eastern Australia. Other similar species are to be seen in such areas as the South of France, which could also grow here and are not easy to discriminate.

69. Lampranthus *Lampranthus roseus*

A different-looking "Mesembryanthemum", being bushy and with short narrow, but fat, leaves. This is a variable species whose flowers can be of many shades of red and pink. It has been put out on cliffs and banks in various places, where it produces fruit, but apparently not seedlings. All the same, the plants survive happily – the clump in this photograph, at Le Gouffre, Guernsey, has since grown much larger and is covered in flower each year. It is a native of South Africa, where it is called Vygie, pronounced fakie.

70. Yellow Pimpernel *Lysimachia nemorum*

Nemorum means of the woods, and it is shady places that this delightful plant likes. It grows in many parts of Britain, but in the Channel
Islands it is to be seen, but rarely, in Jersey and in no other island
except Sark, where it is quite a feature locally, where there are woods.
Now this is a puzzle, for it seems certain that there were no woods at
all in Sark, at least for a long while before it was resettled in late Tudor
times; and then the trees planted were mostly apples, for cider, and
elms. However there it is, happily, a perennial of a different genus
from the other Pimpernels (73).

71. Autumn Squill *Scilla autumnalis*

Autumnalis means, predictably, autumnal – but when does autumn
start? if this plant regulated the calendar, the answer would be in mid-
July; but it is not the only summer-flowerer which bears an autumnal
name. Its congener, the blue-flowered Spring Squill, *S verna*, might
well be expected on geographical grounds to be in the Channel Islands,
but there has never been any report of it. This species is plentiful in
all the islands, abundant indeed in places such as otherwise bare cliff
tops, where its curly leaves can form almost a pure sward on their own.
Squill and *Scilla* (the old name for Bluebells) are the same word, and
both are close relations of the Lilies. This is indeed a miniature Lily

72. Deptford Pink *Dianthus Armeria*

Deptford Pink never did grow in Deptford. The misnomer dates
back to the end of the 16th century, when what was clearly the Maiden
Pink, *D deltoides*, (which also grows in the Channel Islands), was said
to grow there; and in the next edition of this "Herbal", in 1633, an
illustration was added, but of this *D Armeria*. Thus was the error
perpetuated. This is the jewel of a flower to come on on a sunny day in
one of the, few, dry spots in the islands where it occurs, or occurred –
no record yet from Herm. On dull days all that shows are the frankly
leggy stems and thin leaves; and they merge only too readily into the
surrounding grass. So it may be less rare than it seems to be.

70

71

72

73. Scarlet, Pink and Pale Pimpernels *Anagallis arvensis*

Scarlet is the usual, typical, famous indeed, colour of this common annual, a weed of cultivation, perhaps native on the coast. But, especially near the sea, it quite often has pale pink flowers, as in the top of this picture. Much less common is the very pale form at the bottom, which is almost certainly the source of the claim for a white one, which has appeared copied from book to book as the special plant of Jethou. The dried specimen on which the claim is based exists, which seems to deny it, faded though it inevitably is, and a white Pimpernel remains to be found. It is very unusual to see three colour forms growing intermingled, as in this photograph. Blue and wine-coloured forms of this species also occur, but not the always blue *A foemina*, which has its flowers on shorter stalks, and other differences.

74. Bog Pimpernel *Anagallis tenella*

A lovely perennial, not more obviously related to the Scarlet annual than the Yellow (70) is, but botanists see details that others miss. But what matters is that this is a most delicate (hence *tenella*) charmer to be seen in short moist turf in all the islands. When the patch is large, and the flower bells out, the effect is so delightful that it is no wonder that the Royal Horticultural Society gave it an Award of Merit.

75. Slender Cicendia *Cicendia pusilla*

Here is another delightful flower with no proper English name, because people hardly ever notice it. In this instance people may be excused, for it is rarely over 1″ high and at most 4″, and its flowers close when the sun is in. It is in effect a miniature yellow Gentian to be seen in moist slacks and shallow hollows on cliffs, notably in Guernsey, by the diligent who bend low, or kneel. So far it has not been spotted elsewhere, except in Jersey where it is scarce. And where it does grow, other miniatures are likely to grow too, two of them real rarities.

73

74

75

76. Pot Purslane *Portulaca oleracea*

The names of this plant are well connected with the kitchen – *oleracea* implies it comes out of the kitchen garden, and "Pot" plants were used in the cooking pot. "Purslane" is a word applied to almost as many plants as "Samphire". This one is the original, the Mediterranean annual which was given this name by the Romans. It has been widely used as a vegetable in warmer parts, nowadays in improved varieties. But it can also sow itself unduly and uninvitedly, and this it has done for some years in Jersey. In Guernsey it has hardly started, and so far it is not noted from the other islands.

77. Jersey Cudweed *Gnaphalium luteo-album*

A plant long connected with the Channel Islands, having been recorded in Jersey in the 1680's and being known as Jersey Cudweed as far afield as Australia and South Africa. It is now widespread in temperate regions of the world. The original finder called it very common, but that it seems never to have been since. It is very local in the west nowadays, and sporadic in Guernsey. It grows best on moist sandy or gravelly ground, but can also be a weed. The earliest specimen was collected in·Guernsey in the 18th century, but it is so far unrecorded in the other islands except Alderney. The next species is very often mistaken for it.

78. Cape Cudweed *Gnaphalium undulatum*

Cape here means Cape of Good Hope, for this is a South African plant. It had reached north-west France early in the last century, but was not recorded from the Channel Islands until the end of it. Since then it has been spreading there and is now generally frequent and certainly far commoner than the last species. It particularly likes cliffs and waste places, but seems hardly pernickety where it grows. It is to be told from the last by its yellow-green leaves which have an unpleasant odour when rubbed, and by its stems well branched above with many smaller flowers. Jersey Cudweed, when young, sends up just a single simple stem with a cluster of flowers at the top; when it is older, its stems curve typically at the base before going up. Cape Cudweed never so curves – and has not yet been seen in Britain.

76

77

78

79. Giant Echium   *Echium Pininana*

These prominent Rocket Plants sow themselves readily in many a garden in the islands. They form broad leafy rosettes in the first year, and in the second can shoot up to 20′ and more, flower all the summer, and then die. They find conditions so much to their liking that they have even been seen growing in bramble thickets and on the top of a wall. What makes this particularly astonishing is that the only place where this species is native is at 2,000′ in cloud zone laurel forest on La Palma in the Canary Islands. There it is now very scarce, indeed in a precarious state, and prominently numbered among the endangered plants of the world.

80. Vipers Bugloss   *Echium vulgare*

In view of the fact that this is a plant which likes warm dry sandy conditions, one might have expected it to be plentiful in the islands. So it is in Alderney and Herm. But in the others it is as scarce as hens teeth, has indeed not been reported from Jersey and Guernsey for the past ten years, another example of the apparently bizarre distributions of plants and animals locally. The connection with vipers dates back to the 1st century, when the four nutlets of the fruit were said to resemble a vipers head. In America, whither it was transported, it is execrated as Blue Devil, its undeniable beauty notwithstanding.

81. Purple Vipers Bugloss   *Echium plantagineum*

The third member of this genus to be seen in the Channel Islands, but the one recorded there longest of all, for nearly 300 years in Jersey. And today it is in Jersey alone that it is to be found, locally frequently. It was collected in Guernsey for a few years at the end of the last century, but there are no confirmed records from any of the other islands. It is rare in Britain. This too has been exported, very likely on the backs of sheep taken from the Mediterranean to Australia, where it is now a bad weed and called Salvation Jane or Patersons' Curse, the latter after an unfortunate man whose farm was infested with it early on.

79

80

82. Fragrant Evening Primrose   *Oenothera stricta*

All the Evening Primroses are ultimately American – thanks to their special internal breeding mechanisms, variations which arise can get fixed and some of these in Europe are now treated as species. Nearly all the wild ones from North America are rather coarse annuals with, however, large yellow flowers, which may be somewhat fragrant after dark when their pollinators, moths, are on the wing. Commoner than these in the islands and more delicate with more fragrant flowers, which turn coppery when they go over, is this species from South America. Sometimes its stems, leaves and fruits are of a most attractive purplish grey, as in this photograph: a similar form is to be seen in some gardens as 'Moonlight'. It comes true from seed and is much to be encouraged.

83. Tree Lupin   *Lupinus arboreus*

Another plant from America, from the west, which likes sandy places and can cover them with its 4'–5' bushes. Its flowers may also be seen whitish or mauvish. It may also flourish overmuch, causing the local authority to step in and "control" it. But it is far too pleasant to restrict too severely, and the root nodules which it, like all members of the Pea family produce, enrich the poor soils it grows on. It is in all the main islands.

84. Yellow Bartsia   *Parentucellia viscosa*

This viscid plant grows scattered in damp grassy places in most of the islands, as it does in south-west England and Ireland. But it seems to make little impact on most people and has been mistaken for the un-clammy next species and for musk. Its headquarters arc in the Mediterranean.

85. Yellow Rattle   *Rhinanthus minor*

A semi-parasite of grasses in moist meadows, which is not common in the Channel Islands, and known only in the two largest ones. Its English, and local, names allude to the seeds in the bladder-like fruits, which can float. It is at its most appealing in early flower, as in this photograph, when the aptness of another name for it becomes obvious – Chick and Egg Plant.

83

84

85

86. Cabbage Palm   *Cordyline australis*

This is neither a Cabbage, nor a Palm, nor from Australia (*australis* means southern), but New Zealand. It is in fact a member of the Lily family, as the details of its flowers show. These usually grow in such heavy clusters that they hang out of the tufts of leaves at the top of the bare trunks. They are followed by globular white fruits, which sometimes self-sow to give rise to young plants. This is supremely the plant which is supposed to give a "sub-tropical" effect to seaside resorts in the extreme south-west of Britain and is much planted in the Channel Islands.

87. Dew Plant   *Aptenia cordifolia*

Another "Mesem" (67–9), but with much less showy flowers. It was brought over from South Africa, and is used in some parts indoors and for carpet bedding – there is a form with variegated leaves too. It is one of the very few species of its family which is self-fertile. This and its perennial habit have helped it to appear and persist out of doors in Jersey and Guernsey, but a bad frost could kill it. It is naturalised also in the Scillies, the Mediterranean and Australia, where it is called Heart-leaf Ice-plant, or so the books say.

88. Mexican Oxalis   *Oxalis latifolia*

Mexico is indeed where this is native and it too suffers in a cold winter. It is one of three pink-flowered species with trifoliate, clover-like, leaves naturalised in the islands. This one has generally fish-tailed leaflets broadest at the top and spreads by the copious bulbils from its main rootstock. So does Pink Bulbous Oxalis, *O corymbosa*, which has more rounded leaflets broadest about the middle with orange-red spots round the margin underneath. The third pink one, *O articulata*, has a tufted knobbly rootstock and downy rounded leaflets with orange dots scattered all over. The plant in the photograph is disfigured by the Rust *Puccinia oxalidis*, which was first recorded in the British Isles from the Channel Islands in 1973. It has been known there much longer, but no-one had realised it was unreported.

86

87

88

89. Guernsey Fleabane   *Conyza sumatrensis* (*floribunda*)

A dusty weed which few except botanists would notice. But it has a special connection with the Channel Islands in that this species, from South America (despite its Latin name), was first detected there in the British Isles, and as recently as 1960. Nor is it yet known except in Jersey and Guernsey. But these annual American Fleabanes are not easy to tell apart. This one is most like Canadian Fleabane, *C canadensis*, from Canada, which also occurs, and has long hairs on its leaves especially at the edge. The photograph does this plant more than justice, for it is unusually tall and makes the most of its 3′ of height. But it brings out well its typical club-shaped inflorescence. This helps differentiate it from another species which has occurred, *C bonariensis*, from Buenos Aires, whose sideshoots usually overtop the main one.

90. Galingale   *Cyperus longus*

A sort of Sedge, which is rare in Britain, but so attractive with its russet inflorescences that it is planted by ponds, and dries well. In the Channel Islands it is no doubt an ancient native, giving its patois name of Han to certain damp fields. It had many uses. In 1774 it was for saddles. Mats, footstools and collars for draught animals were at the Great Exhibition on 1851; even paper made from it was shown soon after, in Paris. The stems were twisted into cordage for fishing, for tying sheaves and for hobbling animals. Nowadays it is treated as a weed.

91. Green Cyperus   *Cyperus Eragrostis*

A new arrival in the Channel Islands, which has not yet reached Britain, but will hardly have come direct from its native South America. It is another example of a plant once, and maybe still, grown in gardens, which overprospers and gets out. It was found on the banks of the River Loire at Nantes in 1909 and is now common there. It was on the banks of the new reservoir in Guernsey in 1961 and is now plentiful there, and to be seen elsewhere in the island. It was on the banks of the new reservoir in Jersey a few years later, soon after it was completed and is spreading there too. Did birds take it to Jersey?

92. Wild Leek *Allium Ampeloprasum*

An obvious plant, when it is allowed to be obvious. It shows first in early summer as a thick tuft of grey leek-like foliage in roadside banks and hedges. These leaves wither and, in late summer, up come the 5′ or so bare flowering stems with a 2″–3″ ball of flowers at the top, a too attractive bait for stick-whippers. Its distribution is quizzical. It was known from time immemorial on the cliffs south of St Peter Port in Guernsey and nowhere else. In 1904 it was seen on Herm, where no visitor need now spend long finding it. In the late 1920's it was reported, once, in west Guernsey; and since the last war it has suddenly appeared in many places, especially down the west coast and in the south, no-one knows why. In Jersey it has been twice collected and not seen for half a century. It is indeed a wild form of Leek, of a large and complicated group of such Onions to be found chiefly in the Mediterranean area.

93. Autumn Lady's Tresses *Spiranthes autumnalis*

Ichabod, the Glory is gone. Jersey and Guernsey were at one time famous for the Summer Lady's Tresses Orchid, *S aestivalis*, which grew by St Ouen's Pond and in the Grande Mare. But collectors and drainage have made this speciality extinct in the British Isles – it is still to be found in Normandy. Nor can this threnody restore it. Instead there is still its small brother, which appears in short turf near the sea and occasionally on lawns inland just as the summer is ending, fragrant and comely and with its flowers similarly "writhen about the stalk" as a writer in the mid-16th century described it. Nor, happily, is this, yet, rare.

94. Rough Star Thistle *Centaurea aspera*

A doubtful native, but a plant which has been in the three largest islands for a considerable time. It was collected in Guernsey in the 18th century and has been on the west coast ever since, but in ever diminishing quantity. Now there are only three clumps left and these seem to produce no seed. In Jersey it has been known in St Ouen's Bay since the 1830's, and is quite plentiful there. In Alderney a little was found at the end of the last century and there is still a little.

92

93

94

95. Umbellate Hawkweed *Hieracium umbellatum*

This is a special plant, in Jersey and Guernsey at any rate: it needs more study in Alderney; and a rather similar plant, *H bichlorophyllum*, grows in Sark as well as Jersey and Guernsey. Although this photograph shows only the flowers at the top of the stems, in fact there is not much below, for in Jersey and Guernsey it never grows more than some 12″ high: the normal form is often 4′. When experts come to look at this short plant, they find it has a different genetic make-up. It makes a delightful late-flowering plant for a rock garden. It is not common, but there are patches of it on some road and lane-banks, which show up well when the flowers are out.

96. Olearia *Olearia paniculata (Forsteri)*

This is a shrub from New Zealand, named from there as long ago as 1776, much used for hedging, especially in Guernsey. For most of the year all there is to see are tall banks of thick wavy scurfy-grey leaves. These are not unlike those of the attractive, also New Zealand, shrub *Pittosporum tenuifolium* grown in milder parts of the British Isles, including the Channel Islands. The two have totally different flowers. Those of this species are most noticeable when they go over into fluffy fruit. This fruit can and does produce seedlings, which may grow on in waste places. At least two other Olearias are to be seen semi-naturalised in the islands.

97. Wire Plant *Muehlenbeckia complexa*

Another New Zealand shrub, but of very different appearance. This one has very long thin wiry blackish stems which can entangle into complex thickets, smothering hedges and covering old walls, recently measured as reaching nine yards. It bears male and female flowers on different plants – the one in the picture is female with prominent stigmas and the enlarged white sepals showing strikingly. It was introduced in 1842 and depicted in the famous "Botanical Magazine" (started in 1787) from Herm in August 1912. But that colony, near the hotel, has been drastically cut back in recent years.

95

96

97

98. Kangaroo Apple *Solanum laciniatum*

A rare shrubby surprise, with dark purple stems and stalks, which can look after itself outside gardens in the warmest parts of the British Isles. It has done this in Guernsey for half a century, sowing itself and spreading up a bushy hillside. Those actual plants came from New Zealand, but it is native in Australia too. The flowers are fine purple saucers $1\frac{1}{2}''$ or so across, and the fruits ripen an attractive yellow. It has been noted also in Jersey.

99. Belladonna Lily *Amaryllis Belladonna*

This has nothing to do with Belladonna, the Deadly Nightshade, but is what some people call Jersey Lily, although it has no special connection with that island. Jersey Lily was the sobriquet of the Edwardian actress, Lillie Langtry, daughter of a Dean of Jersey. This is a superb plant which throws up in early autumn fine tufts of large flowers on thick, foot high purplish leafless stems. Its bulbs can grow to great size and weight, and prevail against much competition. Consequently they may be seen bursting through in hedges and thickets and waste places in a striking and improbable manner. It comes from South Africa and has been grown in our gardens for 250 years.

100. Guernsey Lily *Nerine sarniensis*

This name has the longest continuous connection with the islands of any flower. It is not a wild plant now: it needs greenhouse protection even in the Channel Islands. And yet, once upon a time it was different. The fable that this reached Guernsey through its bulbs being washed on shore from a shipwreck, where they rooted and flowered on their own, may be safely discounted. But it does seem to have reached he island by 1660 and for the next 150 years to have flourished exceedingly there, and there alone. So much so that by the early 1700's the flowers were being sent in quantity to friends in England, grown in the open. In 1703/4 some were found in a highway, the earliest record for a garden escape, and in 1802 it was said to have been long naturalised in Guernsey. How it fell from this happy state is a mystery. Nor are the few in Guernsey necessarily Guernsey Lilies, for most of those cultivated now are hybrids. But even true Guernsey Lilies vary in colour and otherwise from valley to valley in their native South Africa.

98

99

100

INDEX

References are to the text entries, not to page numbers. Most of the plants are also referred to in the Introduction.